Master Juggling

CASSANDRA BECKERMAN

STERLING INNOVATION
An imprint of Sterling Publishing Co., Inc.

New York / London
www.sterlingpublishing.com

STERLING, the Sterling logo, STERLING INNOVATION, and the Sterling
Innovation logo are registered trademarks of Sterling Publishing Co., Inc.

10 9 8 7 6 5 4 3 2 1

Published by Sterling Publishing Co., Inc.
387 Park Avenue South, New York, NY 10016

© 2009 by Sterling Publishing Co., Inc.

Distributed in Canada by Sterling Publishing
c/o Canadian Manda Group, 165 Dufferin Street
Toronto, Ontario, Canada M6K 3H6

Distributed in the United Kingdom by GMC Distribution Services
Castle Place, 166 High Street, Lewes, East Sussex, England BN7 1XU

Distributed in Australia by Capricorn Link (Australia) Pty. Ltd.
P.O. Box 704, Windsor, NSW 2756, Australia

Printed in China
All rights reserved

Sterling ISBN: 978-1-4027-6587-2

For information about custom editions, special sales, premium and
corporate purchases, please contact Sterling Special Sales Department
at 800-805-5489 or specialsales@sterlingpublishing.com.

Contents

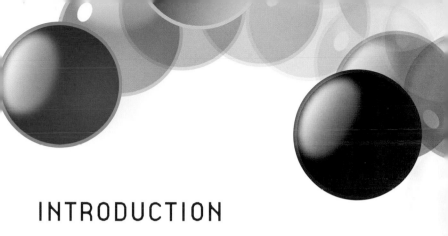

INTRODUCTION

The art of juggling is very familiar to most people. "Juggling" means to keep two or more things in motion at one time. We all do it every day with work, school, family, and our social lives. Picking up a couple of balls and juggling them is really no different than doing homework, making dinner, and watching your favorite TV show all in one evening.

Acts of juggling can be stressful—but the skill becomes easier when you're relaxed. Everyone has had days where everything just goes your way and you are completely free of stress. Then there are other days you'd like to forget. As in life, the more relaxed and calm you are, the easier it will be to juggle, or, in this case, move objects between your hands. Being tense will lead to anxiety and frustration, not to mention a heap of balls on the floor.

It's very easy to break down the art of juggling. It simply requires a couple of objects, skilled hand-eye coordination, and your hands. You already have your hands, eyes, and a brain to put it all together. All you need are the juggling balls in this kit, this book, and you're ready to go. I know that, for me, less has always been more, and the same is true for juggling. The less complicated you make things, the easier it will be to move through the patterns in this book.

Juggling provides an array of benefits that can contribute to your day-to-day life. Believe it or not, juggling is great exercise and develops muscles in your legs, arms, and stomach area. Your reflexes will also become sharper. Juggling helps you to improve your concentration and develop a clear focus. On the lighter side, it adds a lot of fun to your life and can become a great hobby. One thing I have seen over and over again is a building of teamwork with others—you can make lifelong juggling friends. If you decide to be a stage juggler, you will walk away with amazing confidence and dramatic stage presence. All these benefits can be carried with you into other areas of your life.

The skill of juggling has been around for centuries. When we think of jugglers, a medieval court jester or comedic circus clown may come to mind. However, the history of juggling dates as far back as 1900 B.C. One of the first known pictures of juggling is on a panel from the 15th Beni Hassan Egyptian tomb of an unknown prince (c.1994–1781 B.C.). It depicts people juggling balls with one another (Figure 1). This may have been a record from a religious ceremony or a celebration for one of the pharaohs. Other ancient archeological artifacts, including terra cotta statues from Greek and Roman culture, show jugglers at festivals and ceremonies as well. Ancient writings from the East dating back to 475 B.C. demonstrate that juggling was often used to predict the future. Aztec ruins in Mexico show fire juggling used at ceremonies, and juggling dates back to 950 A.D. in the Polynesian Islands, where it was, and still is, considered a sport.

In the Middle Ages (after the fall of the Roman Empire), many jugglers were persecuted because it was thought they were performing a form of witchcraft. It wasn't until the Medieval Era in Europe that juggling became popular in the streets, marketplaces, and as a form of entertainment for royalty. At that time, juggling was called "joge-lean," which comes from Middle English, meaning "to perform or

Figure 1. Art in the Beni Hassan Tomb shows that juggling dates back almost 4000 years.

entertain." In France, jugglers were called "jongleurs," which means "one who jokes." These words derived from the Latin word "joculari," which means "to joke or to jest."

Philip Astley, "Father of the Modern Circus" is attributed with bringing the first juggling acts to the circus. In 1768, he hired jugglers to perform routines as clowns and on horses. These acts became very popular throughout England and France, and later in the United States. Although Astley himself never made it to the U.S., the juggling acts he created and popularized in Europe arrived at the American circus just 25 years later, in 1793. They have been a staple of the circus in the United States ever since.

The 19th century brought the birth of the minstrel music hall shows, a popular form of entertainment in which different types of acts would perform in one complete show—this later became known as vaudeville. These shows featured juggling acts that used plates, balls, knives, pins, and other objects. Many acts included music and incorporated talking to the audience and telling jokes. Salerno and Kara from Germany introduced the gentleman juggler style using hats, canes, and cigar boxes, while the likes of Cinquevalli, Spadoni, and Conchas performed strongman feats that included juggling fire torches and balancing various cannons on the forehead.

By the late 1880s, and into the early 20th century, these acts had transformed into vaudeville. Shows could be seen throughout the United States and Canada. Jugglers often received top billing alongside musical acts, acrobats, dancers, magicians, and comedians. Some famous performers of the time included tramp juggler Chas T. Aldrich, club juggler Harry Lind, and the well-known comedy juggler W.C. Fields.

In the late 1930s, vaudeville began to fade as radio became increasingly popular. Juggling acts died out as well because they simply did not translate to the airwaves as did singers and comedians. With the advent of television, there was a small surge of popularity in variety-act style shows, however during the mid 1940s, juggling became more commonly known as part of the circus or a common pastime.

In 1947, the International Jugglers' Association was created. Since then, it has organized hundreds of conventions across the country. The IJA has helped local juggling clubs to get started, and it is the host of the largest Internet database of juggling information. It even created World Juggling Day, which is held every year in June. Most juggling clubs put on small parties or festivals to celebrate and honor the craft of juggling on that day.

Today, juggling is viewed as something of a specialty variety act. Performances are often seen at fairs, shows, special events, and conventions. Circuses continue to feature legendary juggling acts and there are a wide variety of competitions throughout the world. A subculture of jugglers has been forming for many decades. Many schools and universities have juggling clubs. Private clubs in communities are becoming very common and street juggling has also become accepted in many areas. There is no doubt that the popularity of juggling is on the rise. Who knows, maybe one day it will become an Olympic sport!

JUGGLING BASICS

Juggling involves many different skills and there are a few basic principles you will want to follow for success. This book is designed to break down the skills and teach you specific techniques. Once you have mastered these, you will learn beginning, intermediate, and advanced tricks.

When learning to do anything for the first time, you experience success and failure. Learning to juggle does have many ups and downs—no pun intended! Most people, even professional jugglers, consider juggling an art. You will need to work on and practice your craft to perfect it. Here are a few tips to keep you on track while learning to juggle.

Don't be too hard on yourself. You will drop balls and make mistakes. Allowing yourself room for errors will help you get through the learning process. Juggling is a lot like learning to ride a bike: you just need to keep picking up your juggling balls, like you would your bike, and try, try again.

Train yourself. In order to learn anything new in life, you must train yourself. The way to master these skills is to practice over and over again. You are trying out a new task and it requires you to train your eyes, hands, muscles, and brain. Practicing will prepare you to master these techniques, and soon they will become second nature.

Keep your eye on the ball. Most jugglers agree that the easiest way to juggle is to focus on the balls. What your hands are doing is not an important focus—it may, in fact, distract you. If you use this simple technique, your mind will be free and your hands will train themselves and just fall into place.

Remain tension-free. Being uptight, frustrated, and, above all, tense will only make matters worse. This is something we can all relate to in life. The key to juggling is to remain calm. Try to keep your mind and body loose. When you mess up, just laugh it off and try again. Remember, you're not juggling for the Queen—for now, you're just learning.

Getting Started

There are a few things you will need before getting started on your first juggling lesson. First, take out the three balls provided for you in this kit. These balls are known as *props*. You will want to become familiar with them. Throw them up and catch them to get a feel for the balls and their weight. Repeat this in each hand until you feel comfortable. Try throwing high and low, and from hand to hand, to practice the timing of your catch. Soon you will take these skills and incorporate them to learn the basic three-ball cascade, which is called a *pattern* or *trick*. It is always a good idea to do this throw-and-catch exercise with any object before you begin juggling patterns.

You might not think about this, but comfortable clothing and shoes are very important. Make sure you are able to move around in your clothing and that it will not rip if you have to pick up a couple of dropped balls. There is nothing worse than trying to juggle in high heels or tight pants. Remember: Relaxation and comfort are important to juggling success. Worrying about your clothes and juggling balls at the same time can cause you to become confused and frustrated.

One great thing about juggling is that you can do it almost anywhere, whether at home, school, work, or in the park. When you first learn how to juggle, I recommend that you find a place where you have lots of space so you won't damage anything. Often, juggling students will throw the balls too high or too wide and miss the catch. You don't want to break a window or that antique vase that's been in your family for a century! Practicing in an open space will eliminate any of these kinds of accidents.

Find a juggling friend or two to practice with. There is nothing better than sharing the fun, frustration, and many victories with someone else. You can exchange new ideas and keep each other from picking up bad techniques and habits. Juggling buddies are great and, who knows, you may even start a juggling club together.

Juggling Methods

Many different styles and methods of juggling have been developed over time. Jugglers have created a variety of forms using different objects and effects, and they have incorporated them into a variety of routines.

The most traditional method of juggling is *throwing and catching,* in which objects are thrown and caught without letting them touch the ground. This can be done by one person or two or more people (called *passing*). *Bounce juggling* is a method in which balls are juggled in the air and then bounced on the ground. This offers a great effect for routines.

OBJECT JUGGLING

Using objects is essential to juggling, however I have seen mime jugglers use nothing but air and they are so impressive you'll swear you're seeing balls being moved around in the air. Basically, object juggling is where you pick up two or more items and begin juggling in a catch-and-throw style between your hands. You can juggle solo or with another person as long as you are using some sort of object. Objects may include balls, pins, clubs, scarves, knives, swords, plates, umbrellas, rings, fiery hoops, cigar boxes, fruit, and even chain saws! The list of props you can juggle is endless. Really, you can juggle just about anything as long as you have the skill and a creative imagination.

SPECIALTY OBJECT JUGGLING

Often called *trick juggling*, this is where the objects are put together like mini-juggling kits. Some of the objects may be used as tools to juggle the others—it is different than catch-and-throw juggling. For example, devil sticks are composed of three sticks—one that is juggled in the air by the other two. A diabolo, once used as a kid's toy, is an object you keep spinning on a string while it's suspended between two sticks. Poles or staffs are often juggled around the body while being thrown, twirled, and spun. Another newer form is called *contact juggling*. This involves using clear acrylic balls that are rolled around the hands, arms, chest, head, and legs instead of being traditionally thrown and caught.

Juggling Styles

Juggling styles are commonly associated with the type of juggling performance you are doing. There are four main styles. The first is the *traditional circus style,* which is about precise skill and presentational display. Acrobatic skills, multiple performers, and music are usually incorporated into these acts. The second is called *comedy juggling.*

This is where the performer incorporates jokes, banter, and humor while juggling objects and doing tricks. Often we see these acts performed by a clown or character. Next we have the *gentleman juggler*. The costume usually consists of a suit or formal black-tie look. The juggler uses common objects like walking canes, plates, hats, wine bottles, and cigar boxes. This was a very common vaudevillian style. The last is *strongman juggling*. Always a crowd-pleaser, this involves juggling what appears to be impossible. These acts usually include juggling powered-up chain saws, rings of real fire, and one of the most famous acts—balancing a heavy cannon on the forehead.

Juggling Notation Systems

There are two ways to learn juggling. One is by seeing a juggling pattern demonstrated and then practicing it. The other is by calculating a juggling pattern and recording it. The latter is commonly known in juggling as *notation systems*.

These systems were created because juggling patterns became so complex that tricks needed to be recorded on paper. There are two main types of written notation systems. The most common is known as *siteswap.* This uses numbers to represent different juggling patterns. The other method is *diagram-based* notations, which use drawn images. A new system called *beatmap,* created by Luke Burrage in 2004, makes use of a computer-drawn stick figure of a person juggling balls. This has been very helpful to jugglers who find it easier to learn tricks visually.

SITESWAP

Siteswap notations came into being in the mid-1980s with the creation of new juggling patterns. This is simply a mathematical way of writing a juggling pattern. In siteswapping, a number is used for each throw. If a pattern is indicated by a single number, then this is the simple way of juggling that number of balls. For example, a 3 signifies a three-ball cascade. The number also represents the height and speed of each throw. For instance, a 3 signifies a simple crossing cascade throw, while a 5 represents a higher crossing cascade throw. Numbers also tell us the type of throw: odd numbers represent a cascade that is a cross-throw from one hand to the other, and even numbers represent fountain throws that stay in the same hand. A 1 is a horizontal throw or a straight pass from one hand to the other and seen in shower patterns (a circular motion, demonstrated later in the book). Zeroes denote an empty hand, such as in the 40 pattern, where two balls juggle in one hand while the other is empty. A 2 represents a hold or gap (the ball is not being thrown or caught); for example in a 42, two balls are in one hand while the hold is in the other.

Siteswap Numbers

- 0: Empty hand
- 1: Transfer or pass between hands
- 2: Hold or a gap
- 3: Balls crossing or cascading
- 4: Two balls juggled in one hand
- 5: High throw

Writing a siteswap notation can be like creating a musical pattern. There is a certain rhythm to the pattern and instead of writing it over and over again, such as 51515151, we simply write 51. Notations only work if the sum of all the numbers can be reduced to the number of balls you are throwing. For instance, 51 is a three-ball pattern because $5 + 1 = 6/2 = 3$ (balls). A 52 would not be a valid siteswap pattern as $5+2=7/2=3.5$ (balls). Unfortunately, in juggling we do not juggle half a ball. Here are a few notations; you will learn the techniques as we go on:

Common Three-Ball Siteswap Notations

- 3: Three-ball cascade.
- 51: Classic shower with a straight pass.
- 42: Three-ball shower with simultaneous throws, or Two in One Hand, then hold with the other.
- 441: Fountain from each hand then make a straight pass and repeat on the other side.
- 531: High cascade throw followed by a cross-cascade throw. While the ball is peaking, make a straight pass from the other hand.

What has just been explained in this section is known as *vanilla siteswap*. This is an asynchronous pattern by a solo juggler alternating between the right and left hands. There are other varieties of siteswaps including *multiplex siteswap*, which is for catching, throwing, and/or holding two balls in one hand at the same time; *synch siteswap* where both hands throw at the same time; and *passing siteswap*, which uses more than one juggler. These notations are great for learning and creating new patterns, however they do not give details of how the throws move from right to left and around the body.

DIAGRAM-BASED NOTATIONS

Diagram-based notations are the easiest way to show juggling patterns and how they are moving on paper. They tend to be more detailed than siteswap diagrams because they demonstrate where the throws are coming from and moving to, and in which hands. Many jugglers prefer these diagrams for more complex patterns.

Ladder diagrams are considered the best for tracking the juggling pattern because the diagram follows the path of the balls down the "ladder." These diagrams are read from top to bottom, and each ladder rung represents a beat of time. Recorded on each rung is either a throw, catch, or both, as well as the path of the balls. A black dot signifies a catch. An empty white circle represents throws. The lines demonstrate where the ball is moving from and to. The right side of the ladder is the right hand and the left is the left hand. The top of the ladder shows which balls are in which hands at the start of the pattern (Figure 2).

Some ladder diagrams simply show where the balls are thrown and caught. These diagrams use colors and lines but omit the circles, showing only the flowing paths of the balls that are being juggled (Figure 3).

Causal diagrams are similar to ladder diagrams but they only show where the balls are being juggled. They do not show the balls being caught in the juggler's hands as does the ladder diagram.

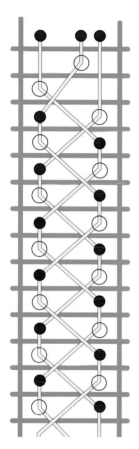

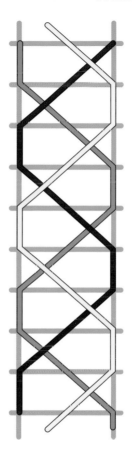

Figure 2. Ladder diagram of the three-ball cascade with key.

Figure 3. A ladder diagram that shows only the paths of the three-ball cascade.

◯ = Throw   ● = Catch

9

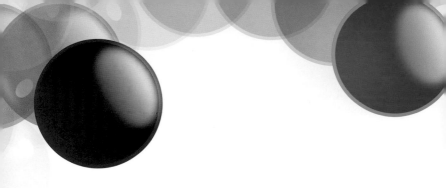

THE THREE-BALL CASCADE

The Three-Ball Cascade is the most basic juggling pattern and the first step in learning to juggle. No one is sure if this was the first juggling pattern, but today it is the first trick most juggling teachers start out with.

Using three balls, the cascade follows a number "8" pattern. As you will see in the following lessons, the ball makes a figure eight moving from your hand to the air to the hand again, and back into the air again. The crossing of the ball in the air to the catch in the hand is what creates the "8." Make sure to read through each section before attempting to juggle, and go back and review the juggling basics if you get frustrated. When you have mastered this technique, you can call yourself a juggler and move on to the beginning, intermediate, and advanced tricks.

Lesson 1: Throwing the Ball

To get a feel for juggling and experience the figure-eight pattern of the Three-Ball Cascade, we will begin simply by throwing one ball from one hand to the other.

Take one of the balls from your juggling kit and hold it in your dominant hand (for most, this is the right hand). Make sure to keep your body relaxed, knees slightly bent, and breathe. With elbows close to your waist, keep your arms extended out in front of you with both palms up. Now, as you throw the ball from one hand to the other, you want to scoop from the outside to the inside, making the top of a figure eight (Figures 4 and 5). Then release the ball, throwing it to the other hand. When you catch it on the other side, repeat the figure-eight scoop and throw it back.

Ideally, each time you throw the ball, it should peak overhead at the center of your body. Throw the ball

Figure 4. Begin the Three-Ball Cascade by throwing one ball from hand to hand.

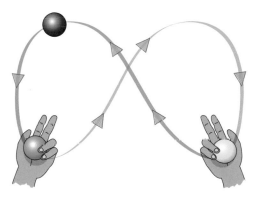

Figure 5. Juggle the balls so they create a figure-eight in the air.

11

slightly inward when tossing, and catch it slightly outward in your palm at waist level. You will notice that the action of this pattern takes place in a circular space. You should juggle the balls in the target zone between waist and above the head. Try throwing gently with precision. This will help you create a steady rhythm, making the figure-eight pattern flow smoothly.

Practice over and over again until you are comfortable. When you feel in control and have mastered a rhythm with one ball, you are ready to move on to the next lesson.

Lesson 2: Transferring Two Balls

For this lesson, we will simply add another ball into our cascading figure eight and transfer the balls back and forth. Keep in mind that this exchange moves a lot faster, and there will be more trial and error than in lesson 1. The following pointers will help, as does practice.

Take two balls from your juggling kit and place one in each hand. We will be using the same figure-eight techniques as lesson 1, however we will now have two balls in motion instead of one. For our purposes let's say the ball in the right hand is ball A and the one in the left hand is ball B.

Throw ball A from your right hand to your left hand. Now comes the tricky part: As ball A crosses its peak overhead and is about to land in your left hand, throw ball B to your right hand. Ball B should cross under ball A and overhead as well. The balls should wind up in opposite hands. Repeat this back-and-forth exchange until you can continuously transfer the balls without stopping or dropping them (Figure 6).

POINTERS

RELAX: There is nothing worse than being tense, especially when performing a hand-eye coordination movement. Relax your shoulders, arms, and stomach. Keep your knees slightly bent and loose, and breathe from your belly. Clear your mind and release any tension you are holding in your jaw. This will help you to avoid being stiff and tense.

Figure 6. Throw two balls from hand to hand.

MASTER THE FORM: In learning the proper form, you want to throw the balls inward toward your center. If you throw them outward, you will end up chasing them away from you. To throw inward, imagine the center of your body remaining still, knees bent, and all movement coming from your arms and hands. Toss the ball with small controlled and precise movements within the parameters of your waist-to-overhead area. This prevents you from lunging forward to catch the balls.

FOCUS: As you exchange the balls, focus on the movement in the air and not on your hands, except for throwing the ball. Your focus should *not* be on catching the ball nor on anything else that is going on around you. This is a little trick that helps to relax your mind and reduce panic.

PERFECT YOUR PACE AND TIMING: You will want to practice a regular pacing and timing of your throws until they become consistent every time. You can even count your throws such as 1-2-3, 1-2-3, or pace them like the beat to music. Pacing really helps to keep the pattern moving and reduces dropped balls.

PRACTICE, PRACTICE, PRACTICE: Need I say more! Juggling is a process and could cause you to become frustrated and feel like giving up. When practicing, allow yourself to fail and just laugh off any errors. Even professional jugglers have to practice their craft.

YOU'VE GOT IT!: Most jugglers know they have mastered a trick when they can do it consistently a certain number of times in a row. For simple tricks like the cascade, it is usually 20 times; for complex tricks like Above the Head, it is 10 times. Anything that involves using the body, such as Behind the Back or Under the Knee should be done 5 times.

Lesson 3: Completing the Three-Ball Cascade

By now, you have mastered throwing two balls and may even be performing for your family and friends. You are ready to cascade a figure eight of three balls and call yourself a juggler.

Take all three balls from your juggling kit. Place two balls in your right hand (we'll call them balls A and C) and place the last ball (B) in your left hand. Throw ball A to your left hand. As it crosses eye level, throw ball B to your right hand. Catch ball A in your left hand. Here is the tricky part: As you are catching ball A in your left, you will throw ball C from your right hand to your left. Catch ball B with your right hand. As ball C is landing in your left hand, start the whole cycle again, throwing ball A from your left (Figure 7).

There are a couple of things to remember when juggling three balls. First, only one ball is in the air at a time when you are performing the Three-Ball Cascade. The other two balls are in the right and left hands and are waiting to be thrown as soon as the one in the air peaks above your head at center and is ready to land. Never throw out of the same hand twice. Always throw right-hand (your dominant hand), then left, and so on. You want to think of the balls as simply cascading around a figure eight from air to hand to air to hand. As in lesson 2, keep practicing until you have a rhythm and flow. You may even want to time yourself and see how long you can juggle for. If you have problems, go back to lesson 2 and read over the Pointers for help. Now that you have mastered the Three-Ball Cascade, move on to the next section, which will teach you other basic juggling tricks.

Figure 7. Throw three balls from hand to hand.

BEGINNING
JUGGLING TRICKS

Most jugglers would agree that once you learn the Three-Ball Cascade, it is pretty easy to master most basic juggling tricks. Many of these patterns are just variations of the Three-Ball Cascade. More advanced tricks usually take practice because they are more complex, but as you will see, they are a lot easier when you master the basics.

Learning new tricks will make the art of juggling more exciting. Let's face it, juggling only the cascade can get pretty boring after a while. Once you have learned the patterns in this section, you can begin to put them together. Combining two or more tricks is how you begin to make a routine. This is how the professionals do it and you can too.

If you really want to get good at juggling, try setting aside 10 minutes a day to practice. The great thing is that once you have your movements under control, you can take out your juggling balls and juggle just about anywhere. You'll be amazed by how good you can become in one week or a month.

The following basic juggling tricks are meant for beginners. Make sure to read over each trick before attempting it. Use the photos to guide you. Remember to go back and review the Pointers in the Three-Ball Cascade section if you have problems. Those key points are great for eliminating frustration. The same guidelines apply when beginning to learn any new tricks.

Two in One Hand

You need to know: None

This is a basic trick that many juggling teachers start out with before even teaching the three-ball cascade. It will probably be very simple since you have mastered the cascade. The Two in One Hand is commonly used in many four-ball juggling tricks.

Instructions: To begin, take two balls in one hand and allow the other hand to rest at your side or place it on your hip. Simply toss ball A into the air. When it peaks, throw ball B and catch ball A. Then repeat the toss with ball A.

Tips: Make sure the hand you are not using stays out of the way. Some jugglers put it behind their back, which creates balance. Remember the column goes up and down in a line pattern while the shower moves in a circle.

Two in One Hand: Column

There are two throw variations for the Two in One Hand trick. The first is called the column. In this trick, the ball simply moves up and down in a straight line.

Instructions: To do the column, throw the ball straight up and down as if it is moving along a linear column. Be sure to throw straight up to eye level without throwing to the outside or inside of the body. This creates a parallel throw and looks as if the ball is traveling up and down like an elevator (Figure 8).

Two in One Hand: Shower

The other throw variation for the Two in One Hand trick is called the shower. Instead of up and down like the column, the balls will move in a circular motion between the hand and air (Figure 9).

Instructions: Begin by throwing ball A in a circular clockwise motion to the outside of the body. When it peaks at eye level, throw ball B in the same direction. This creates an arc for a circle throw. This is the basis for all shower patterns.

Figure 8. The Two in One Hand column

Figure 9. The Two in One Hand shower

Reverse Cascade

You need to know: Three-Ball Cascade

Many find this variation of the Three-Ball Cascade to be easier than the three-ball cascade itself. Simply put, it is a reversal of the cascade. Instead of throwing the balls inside toward your center, you will be throwing them to the outside of your hands (Figure 10).

Instructions: Take three balls in your hands like you would if starting the three-ball cascade—balls A and C in your right hand and ball B in your left. Throw ball A in an arc-like motion to the outside of your right side. Make sure you thrust the ball with force so that it travels up and over your head; you want the ball to peak at the center of your body and begin to fall from there. As ball A peaks inward toward your

center, throw ball B in an arc-like motion to the outside of your left side. Catch ball A with your left hand and as ball B peaks at your center, throw ball C in an arc-like motion to the outside of your right hand. Catch ball B in your right hand and as ball C peaks at your center, begin the sequence again.

Tips: The key to the reverse cascade is to throw the balls in outside circles and have them fall at the center of your body.

Figure 10.
The Reverse Cascade

19

Juggler's Tennis

You need to know: Three-Ball Cascade, Reverse Cascade

This is a great trick to learn after the Three-Ball Cascade and Reverse Cascade. For most jugglers, it is considered an easy variation. Even though this pattern will look like a tennis match, the word *tennis* in juggling refers to an over-the-top throw. In layman's terms, this is thrown high over the head, well above eye level (Figure 11).

Figure 11. Juggler's Tennis

Instructions: Before you begin, pick one ball and call it A. Ball A will be doing the tennis part of the juggle. Start by juggling the Three-Ball Cascade. When you are ready, throw ball A in a circular motion like the Reverse Cascade; as you throw to the outside, toss the ball up and over the other two balls in an over-the-top throw. When you catch ball A, go back to the three-ball cascade for the next two throws. On the third throw, repeat the over-the-top throw with ball A on the other side followed by two cascade throws.

Tips: The over-the-top throw on each side creates a back-and-forth effect that looks like you are juggling a tennis game with ball A. Sometimes jugglers will toss the over-the-top throw wide, creating a bigger tennis-like effect.

The Shower

You need to know: Three-Ball Cascade

The Shower is often considered to be a big circular motion of juggling. This is where one hand throws and the other hand catches (Figure 12). This move uses a quick hand-off pass motion. Many clowns use the shower in their acts.

Figure 12. The Shower

Instructions: Like in the Two in One Hand shower pattern, you will want the balls to move in an arc-like circular pattern. Start with balls A and C in your right hand and ball B in your left hand. Throw ball A up to catch it in the left hand. When it reaches its peak above the head, throw ball C from your right hand. Quickly, pass ball B (in your left hand) across to your right while the other two are in the air. Catch ball A with your left hand and quickly pass it to your right hand before you catch ball C. Repeat the pattern again.

Tips: Note that when doing this trick, the right hand is always throwing and the left hand is always catching and passing. The shower can only move in one direction at a time— clockwise or counterclockwise. This pattern requires a steady pace and quick speed.

21

The Half-Shower

You need to know: Three-Ball Cascade, The Shower, Juggler's Tennis

The Half-Shower is just a slight varia-tion of The Shower. It is a called a *Half*-Shower because half of the time one hand makes throws from the out-side while, half of the time, the other hand throws from the inside. This also creates high and low throws because throws from one hand are thrown over the throws from the other hand (Figure 13).

Instructions: Start juggling the shower pattern. When you are ready, throw one ball to the outside of your body like in juggler's tennis or the reverse cascade. Make sure the ball moves up and over the other two balls. Now repeat that throw every time and continue to shower.

Figure 13. The Half-Shower

Tips: Make sure not to throw the reverse throw too high.

The Claw

You need to know: Three-Ball Cascade

The Claw is basically the Three-Ball Cascade with a different technique of catching the ball. Instead of juggling with your palms up and letting the balls fall, you will juggle with your palms forward and claw the ball out of mid-air. I like to think of a bear holding up its paws and clawing the balls as it juggles. This technique is used in many juggling tricks and routines.

Instructions: It is best to practice the claw technique with one ball first. Take a ball in your palm, throw it up, and snatch it out of the air with your palm facing forward (Figure 14). Try this a few times with both hands until the claw motion becomes comfortable (Figure 15). When you are ready, pick up all three balls and hold them like you are about to juggle a Three-Ball Cascade. As your first ball peaks, claw it out of the air instead of letting it fall, and do this with the rest of the balls. The tough part is that all the throws must be made from the claw position as well.

Figure 14. Claw one ball out of the air.

Tips: Throw the ball high from the claw position so that when you are juggling the balls, they won't travel towards the floor. Keep a very fast and steady pace during this pattern.

Figure 15. Practice The Claw until you become comfortable.

INTERMEDIATE
JUGGLING TRICKS

Many of these intermediate patterns are variations of tricks you already learned in the beginning section, however, these require more skill and will incorporate different movements around the body. Audiences love these more advanced tricks. Take them slowly. Many of these tricks may take a few hours or even a few days to master.

Above the Head

You need to know: Three-Ball Cascade

As the name indicates, you will attempt to juggle three balls above your head. This requires a different position of the hands and can make your triceps sore. This trick is entertaining and often elicits lots of audience applause. Once you have learned how to juggle above the head, you can try juggling other tricks above the head as well.

Instructions: As you can see in the picture, you will be juggling a Three-Ball Cascade overhead (Figure 16). Note that your arms will take a different position. Also, instead of the balls making a figure-eight across your body, they will make small crosses above your head. Place the balls in your hands above your head with palms facing upward toward the sky. Now as you begin to juggle, push the balls upward as if you are popping them like popcorn. Make sure to use smaller crosses with the balls than you would if juggling a standard three-ball cascade.

Figure 16. Above the Head

Tips: Keep your elbows bent and point them outward from the head at about neck level. Forearms should stay up in the air while juggling the balls on your palms. Do not lock your knees—keep them loose or bend them slightly.

Three-Ball Flash

You need to know: Three-Ball Cascade

In juggling, the word "flash" has two different meanings. The first describes the number of throws or catches in a pattern. For example, the three-ball cascade would be catch, catch, and catch. The second meaning refers to throwing all the balls up in the air so your hands can be free for a beat or even two before you catch again. In the three-ball flash, you will be using what is called a high throw or "flash" to create that hands-free beat.

Instructions: Start out by juggling a regular Three-Ball Cascade pattern. Beginning on the third repetition, throw the balls very high overhead (the high throw). This will create a gap of space or beat before the balls fall back down into the hands (Figure 17). After catching the balls, repeat the pattern.

Tips: Here are a few spectacular variations to incorporate into this trick. When you make the high throw or "flash," try clapping your hands. If you find this to be easy, try clapping your hands in front of and then in back of you while the balls are in mid-air. When this skill becomes easy, try turning around and doing a pirouette while all the balls are high overhead (Figure 18). Then catch all the balls and resume juggling.

Figure 17. The basic Three-Ball Flash

Figure 18. Add a pirouette to the Three-Ball Flash for stunning effect.

Columns

You need to know: Two in One Hand

We previously learned to juggle columns with the Two in One Hand juggle. Now you will learn to do columns with three balls. As before, the balls will be moving straight up and down like a column in a synchronized manner (Figure 19). The balls do not cross each other as in the three-ball cascade.

Instructions: First, go back to the technique of juggling two balls in one hand. Practice this in both the right and left hands. When you feel confident, continue with the instructions, adding a third ball.

Figure 19. Columns with three juggling balls

Put ball A and C in your right hand and ball B in your left hand. Throw ball A up. When it peaks, throw ball C and B up at the same time. Catch ball A with your left. Throw ball A again, then simultaneously catch balls C with the right hand and B with the left hand. Throw balls C and B and catch ball A with the right hand. Basically, you are throwing balls C and B up and down like continuous columns, catching and throwing in the same hands. Ball A is also thrown like a column, but it moves through the center, is caught with the right hand, then the left, and repeated.

Tips: Both hands move together and throw at the same time.

Fake Columns

You need to know: Two in One Hand, Columns

Some people find juggling fake columns easier to accomplish than regular columns. In this trick, you are basically performing Two in One Hand while moving the third ball up and down in the other hand (Figure 20).

Instructions: Begin by juggling Two in One Hand. Place the third ball in the opposite hand. As one of the balls in the first hand travels up into the air, move the hand holding the third ball up and down in sync with the other ball. This ball (which is not being juggled) will never be thrown during the pattern. Repeat as the next ball is thrown.

Tips: Make sure you are throwing the balls in a linear column. The ball moving up and down should be even with the ball being thrown.

Figure 20. Fake Columns

Yo-Yo

You need to know: Two in One Hand, Columns, Fake Columns

This trick looks like you are making the balls travel up and down like a yo-yo (Figure 21). This is just a variation on the column theme—it's not too difficult and it gets audience applause every time.

Instructions: Place balls B and C in the right hand and ball A in the left. Please note that ball A will never be tossed; it simply stays in the left hand, which will move up and down like a yo-yo. Make sure to hold ball A with your palm facing down. As you move your hand up and down, you'll want it to look as if you are pulling the ball up and pushing it down. Now start juggling the Two in One Hand column with balls B and C. Make sure you catch to the right and then to the left. Here is the part that makes this pattern look like a yo-yo: ball B's placement should be moving up and down on the left

Figure 21. The Yo-Yo

side where ball A is. As your left hand goes up and down, make sure ball B also moves up and down directly under your left hand.

Tips: Imagine a yo-yo string between ball A and B that holds the two together as you juggle them up and down. Go over the fake column (described at the end of "Columns") to juggle balls B and C.

Chops

You need to know: Three-Ball Cascade, The Claw

Chops are another variation on the Three-Ball Cascade that uses advanced underarm throws and the claw hand placement. Instead of snatching the ball out of the air like the claw, you will be throwing the ball from the claw position. This is a trick that may take a lot of practice and a few days to master (Figure 22).

Instructions: We will use two steps to learn this trick.

Start juggling the three-ball cascade. When you are ready, make an underarm throw by reaching across the other arm. You may have to move the other arm out of the way a bit. Once you are comfortable with this, try the underarm throw every time.

Now you are ready for the chops part. Every time you throw underarm, catch the ball with a chop-like movement. The chopping hand should be catching the ball in a claw-like position with the arm facing straight up next to your ear. Once you catch the ball, bring it down and throw it under the arm and repeat this on the other side.

Figure 22. Chops

Tips: Make sure your catches are high by the side of the head, near your ear. Make a chopping motion as you grab the ball, and move it down for the underarm throw. Make sure that when you throw under the arm, the ball also goes high by the side of your head. This is a common trick jugglers use with clubs.

High and Low Shower

You need to know: The Shower

This trick can be done with three or more juggling balls. As its name indicates, you juggle a low shower pattern under a high shower pattern (Figure 23). Timing is everything on this trick.

Instructions: Begin by juggling a traditional Three-Ball Shower and every so often throw a high ball. When the high one is about to peak above your head, make a small exchange shower below. Catch your high ball and do a low shower before repeating the high throw and low shower exchange below.

Tips: Throw high and exchange the low balls quickly so you have enough time to catch the high ball.

Figure 23. High and low Shower

ADVANCED JUGGLING TRICKS

Advanced juggling requires more skill and concentrated focus. Again, practice and time will be important as you learn these tricks. These are more complex variations of the tricks you have already mastered and may incorporate other props and specific body movements. I like to think of these tricks as dramatic crowd pleasers that can be added to any routine.

Behind the Back

You need to know: Three-Ball Cascade

In this very flashy trick, you will be twisting and juggling the ball around your body (Figure 24). It is not hard to do, but it does take some practice to master the skill and timing of the back throw. If you have a bad back, I would recommend skipping this one.

Instructions: It's best to practice the back throw with one ball first. Take ball A and, as you slightly bend backwards, throw the ball, releasing it somewhere around the lower middle of your back. You'll want the ball to follow over your shoulder and then you'll catch it. Practice this on both sides until you feel comfortable with the timing. Now start out juggling the Three-Ball Cascade, and every couple of throws try one Behind the Back maneuver, then continue cascading and repeat.

Tips: Make sure you throw the ball behind your back high enough to go over your shoulder. If you get really good at this trick, try back-crosses. This is where you do consecutive back throws, that is, you cross behind your back every time you catch and throw without stopping to do a cascade. This can look as if you are juggling the cascade behind your back. Most beginning jugglers can only do this a few times.

Figure 24. Behind the Back

Under the Knee

You need to know: Three-Ball Cascade, Behind the Back

For some, Under the Knee is considered an intermediate trick, but I have categorized it as advanced because it does take precise skill, coordination, and balance on one leg to do it right. Like the name states, you will be juggling one ball under the knee (Figure 25). Please do not try this trick if you have a bad back or knee problems.

Instructions: Start out by juggling the Three-Ball Cascade. After a few times, simply make your throw by lifting one of your legs and catching the ball in front of your center, then continue juggling. After about three cascades, repeat again. You can use the same knee every time or you can alternate knees.

Tips: Make sure to raise the knee high enough so the ball can pass smoothly. Aim your throw up to your center for the catch. You can also do this trick consecutively, however, I would only recommend four or five times so you don't lose your balance or get fatigued.

Figure 25. Under the Knee

35

Over the Shoulder

You need to know: Three-Ball Cascade, Behind the Back

Simply stated in its name, this pattern involves a ball thrown over the shoulder, caught, and then juggled into a Three-Ball Cascade (Figure 26). This trick can be awkward; it requires the torso to move in unnatural ways. The challenging part is that you will have to catch the ball coming over your shoulder without looking. Please do not try this trick if you have a bad back or neck problems.

Instructions: First start out by taking one ball, throwing it up and over your shoulder, and catching it with the opposite hand just behind you by your side. You will have to execute a slight body twist to make the blind catch behind you. When you catch the ball, bring it forward, throw it over the other shoulder, and repeat. Practice this a few times until you become comfortable.

Figure 26. Over the Shoulder

Now, start out by cascading three balls. Pick a ball A. When ready, toss ball A over the shoulder and keep cascading the other balls. Catch ball A, bring it forward, throw it over the other shoulder again, and repeat the cascade.

Tips: Remember this is a blind catch so you will have to trust yourself and feel when to catch the ball rather than looking at it. Twisting the torso and looking up at the ball as it is thrown makes a spectacular presentation for audiences.

The Snake

You need to know: Three-Ball Cascade, The Shower

The Snake is very commonly used in five-ball juggling. Incorporating the cascade and shower techniques, the balls follow each other to make a snake-like pattern (Figure 27). This trick is very pleasing to the eye and exciting to all.

Instructions: To do the snake, you will cascade the three balls and take a beat on each side to shower two of the balls in between the cascade. Start out by juggling the Three-Ball Cascade. Now, shower two balls in the right hand while the other ball is peaking over your forehead. Catch and then repeat by showering two balls in the left hand. The shower in between the cascade makes it look like a snake is chasing its tail.

Figure 27. The Snake

Tips: When you start to shower the two balls, throw the other ball high just above your forehead for timing. If you are having trouble, try this: Place all three balls in the right hand, throw ball A, then B, then C, and catch them in a 1, 2, 3 timing in the other hand. This will help you perfect the shower timing.

Eating an Apple

You need to know: Three-Ball Cascade

I love this trick because it makes use of another type of prop and, if done correctly, is definitely an audience favorite. You will use two balls and an apple for this trick. While juggling the Three-Ball Cascade, you will attempt to take a bite out of the apple. Many jugglers and clowns use this trick in comedy routines. It looks easy but it does take practice and, of course, a big bag of apples.

Instructions: Before using an actual apple you will want to practice with three balls. Start by juggling the Three-Ball Cascade and pick one of the balls to be your apple. Throw one ball extra high. While that ball is high in the air, kiss the ball that you picked as the apple—it should be in one of your hands (Figure 28). Then catch the one in the air. Continue the cascade and repeat the trick again. You'll want to kiss the ball for a quick second on every third juggle. Keep practicing until you get the timing down. When you are ready for the apple, start out by using the kiss technique with two juggling balls and kiss the apple. When you're ready, try taking a bite (Figure 29). Do this on the third cascade juggle.

Figure 28. Practice the technique by kissing the apple first.

38

Tips: Remember to throw high when you are going to eat the apple. This will give you time to take a bite. Make sure the apple is clean, the stem removed, and there are no bugs. The apple will become wet and sticky if you take a lot of bites. Keep plenty of apples on hand to practice with, and make sure to clean your hands and the juggling balls when they get wet and sticky.

Figure 29. When you have the timing down, you can take a bite out of the apple.

Mills Mess

You need to know: Three-Ball Cascade, Reverse Cascade, Chops (underarm cross)

This is an advanced trick that, once mastered, will move you into the category of advanced or even professional juggler. Created by Steve Mills, this trick at first seems like one big chaotic mess but it actually puts three simple tricks together. Basically it is the Cascade, Reverse Cascade, and the underarm pattern of Chops. This trick may take some time to learn.

Instructions: For learning purposes, we will break this trick into four stages. If you get confused when moving on, go back and practice the previous section until you have it down.

Begin with one ball, practicing the chops underarm movement (Figure 30). Place the ball in your right hand and cross it under your left hand. Throw the ball in a rainbow-like arc. Uncross your hands and move the left hand to catch the ball. Move your left hand under your right arm and make a rainbow throw. Uncross your arms and catch with the right and repeat. When this is effortless, move on to the next step.

Figure 30. Begin by tossing one ball using the underarm movement.

We will now practice a variation of the Reverse Cascade. Holding your arms in an open position, throw the ball from your left hand straight up like a column. Before the ball falls, move your right hand under your left and catch the ball in your right hand (Figure 31). Open your arms so they are uncrossed. Throw the ball straight up like a column from the right hand. Cross your left hand under your right and catch the ball with your left hand. Uncross your arms and start again. Note that you are crossing and uncrossing your arms—the ball does not cross. It is thrown and caught in a column throw. When you have gotten used to this pattern, move on.

Place one ball in your right hand and cross both arms with the left arm on top of the right. Throw the ball straight up like a column and uncross your arms (Figure 32). Catch the ball in your left hand with

Figure 31. Toss one ball from the outside of the body while crossing your arm under to catch.

Figure 32. Toss the ball column-style.

your arms in an open position. To repeat on the other side, cross your arms with the right hand on top and throw the ball column-style from your left hand. Uncross your arms and catch the ball in your right hand. To repeat again, carry the ball across and under your left hand. Then repeat the whole routine from the beginning. When you have this technique down, move on to the final step.

Now let's put the three previous steps together. Breaking it down, we will execute the under-the-arm Chops movement, Reverse Cascade, and the Reverse Cascade with crossed arms. Begin the Three-Ball Cascade. When ready, cross the right hand under the left arm and throw rainbow style. As you uncross your arms to the open position, throw the second ball from your left hand, rainbow style. Cross your arms right over left (Figure 33). Toss the ball from the right hand and move your arms to the open

Figure 33. The full technique will take a bit of practice.

position. Repeat. You should have completed three consecutive throws on the left starting with the right hand and catching each ball in the opposite hand that it was thrown from. It's as if three balls snake around one side and then move to the other side.

Tips: As you cascade, remember balls are thrown and caught from a crossing position or an uncrossed open-arm position. The balls follow a path and rhythm that is continuous throughout the trick. Balls are thrown from one hand and caught in the other.

Neck-Catch Finish

You need to know: Three-Ball Cascade, High Shower

The Neck Catch is often used at the end of a routine. It can be done from almost any pattern. This does take a full body movement. Very simply, you will throw the ball high and catch it on the back of your neck. If you have a bad back, I would advise not attempting this one.

Instructions: It is good to practice the Neck Catch from the Three-Ball Cascade, however you can perform this trick from any of the other patterns. Start cascading the balls. Throw one ball very high, watching it. As it starts to fall, bend down with a straight back, keeping your head up, and catch the ball right behind your neck. Keeping your head up creates a groove, and that's where you want to catch the ball. In a variation of this trick, you use the back of your neck to throw the ball over your shoulder with the same jolting momentum you would use from your hand. Then as you stand up, grab the ball and continue juggling the cascade. On about the third cascade, throw the ball high, catch it on your neck, and repeat.

Tips: When performing this trick at the end of a routine, hold it a moment for applause, then thrust the ball up from your neck and catch it in your hand so you can take a bow. When you bend over, try to hold your position in an "L" shape with a flat back. Do not lock your knees. If you are juggling from your neck, pause for a moment

Figure 34. The Neck Catch is a
great way to wind up your routine.

or take a beat when you catch the ball with your neck. A variation
is to complete the bow by dropping to one knee (Figure 34). Then
continue the throw and cascade. That beat makes for a dramatic effect
and usually you will get audience applause.

JUGGLING FOUR
AND FIVE BALLS

Juggling more than three balls can seem like a challenge. However, most four- and five-ball juggling patterns are simply variations of three-ball tricks with additional juggling balls. When trying these patterns, you will have to apply more focus and concentration, as well as speeding up the pace. If you have become proficient at the beginning, intermediate, and advanced tricks, four- and five-ball juggling should be easy. It simply requires a little more practice and patience.

Four-Ball Fountain

You need to know: Two in One Hand, Columns

"Fountain" is a basic term that refers to juggling an even number of balls. The Four-Ball Fountain incorporates the Two in One Hand technique, using both hands at the same time. The balls never cross each other; they move in an up and down motion (Figure 35).

Instructions: Start out by juggling two balls in one hand and then practice on the other side. When you are comfortable, place two balls in the right hand and two balls in the left hand. Begin juggling Two in One Hand on one side only. When one of the balls is at peak eye level, begin throwing Two in One Hand with the opposite hand. Make sure the columns you are juggling are not in sync with each other. This technique prevents the balls from colliding with each other.

Tips: Make sure you are throwing the balls in a linear column pattern. Focus on what the balls are doing in the air and not on your hands.

Figure 35. The Four-Ball Fountain

Four-Ball Shower

You need to know: The Shower

The Four-Ball Shower is just the Three-Ball Shower with an additional ball (Figure 36). This may seem easy but this trick requires speed and steady pacing

Instructions: Start out with three balls in one hand and one in the other. Start throwing the three balls up, and make sure they are a little higher than a typical Three-Ball Shower. When all of the balls are in the air, pass your fourth ball and start catching the other ones.

Begin passing those balls and repeat the cycle. Keep the momentum going and don't forget to throw high above your head.

Tips: Make sure to throw above the head with the ball peaking at your center. Keep a circular motion during the trick. This helps with speed and pace.

Figure 36. The Four-Ball Shower

Five-Ball Cascade

You need to know: Three-Ball Cascade, Four-Ball Fountain

This is a trick that will stun your audience and make you look like a professional juggler. It seems easy at first, but this one really does take some skill and practice. I like to think of this trick as two three-ball cascades or figure eights chasing each other while being juggled at the same time (Figure 37).

Instructions: There aren't a lot of instructions for this technique except to make sure you really know the Four-Ball Fountain before attempting this trick. Start with three balls in one hand and two in the other, and begin juggling the Three-Ball Cascade. Make sure to throw the balls high, just over your head, so that when you have three balls about to peak, you can throw the other two. Move the balls fast and cross them high in the air throughout the trick.

Tips: Move fast without panic and make sure to have three balls moving in the air at one time. Assume a firm stance with your legs and keep your knees slightly bent for balance.

Figure 37. The Five-Ball Cascade

Five-Ball Shower

You need to know: Five-Ball Cascade, Four-Ball Fountain

The Five-Ball Shower is another crowd-pleasing trick. Just like the Half-Shower, you will be making a circular pattern with the Juggler's Tennis throw that moves high over the head (Figure 38). As with the previous tricks, this one requires a lot of speed and a steady pace.

Instructions: Start out with three balls in one hand and two in the other. Begin throwing the three in high flash throws; when they are above your head, pass one of the balls and throw it. As you are about to catch the first ball coming down, pass the last ball and toss it with a high flash throw as well. Make sure to throw the balls to the outside of your body with the high flash throw. This will create the circular shower motion.

Figure 38. The Five-Ball Shower

Tips: Remember that one ball is being thrown and one ball is always being caught. Throw high and to the outside. Again, move with a steady pace.

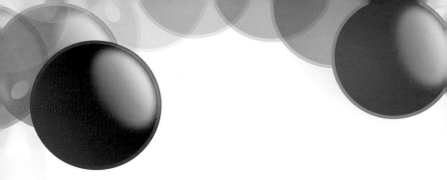

INDEX